52 BIBLE VERSES FOR NEW BELIEVERS

fifty two devotionals to build your faith

SAMUEL DEUTH

ISBN-978-1-64744-138-8

Printed in the United States of America

Published by Outreach, Inc. Colorado Springs, CO 80919
www.Outreach.com

Interior Design by Alexia Garaventa

BEFORE YOU BEGIN

These fifty-two Bible verses will build the foundation for your relationship with Jesus and release you into a future full of life, purpose, and impact!

You can go through the book daily and read it multiple times in a year, or you can read each verse for a week and memorize it before moving on to the next verse.

As you read each verse and devotional, be sure to take the time to ask and answer the questions. The power of God's Word is in the application of its truths.

Included with each verse is a confession of faith section. These declarations are based on the Bible verse; they will transform your mind and guide your life!

FOR MORE DEVOTIONAL RESOURCES

DOWNLOAD THE

FOLLOWING JESUS APP

1

"In the beginning God created the heavens and the earth. Now the earth was formless and empty, darkness was over the surface of the deep, and the Spirit of God was hovering over the waters. And God said, 'Let there be light,' and there was light."

Genesis 1:1-3

DEVOTION

These few verses give us confidence and clarity about our Creator and our intentional design. Many people live life confused and void of meaning because they're looking for life's answers everywhere but the Source. When you need answers and help, go to the Author and Creator; no one else can better lead and inform you. God is the all-powerful Creator, and He also chooses to be with us and invites us to connect and communicate with Him. God is powerful, and He's also very present in this moment with you!

QUESTIONS

Have you considered how incredible creation is? Have you stopped to thank God for life and all He's created? Have you gone to Him with your questions?

CONFESSION

There is one true God! He made the heavens and the earth. By His Word, He created everything we see.

2

"Then God said, 'Let us make mankind in our image, in our likeness, so that they may rule over the fish in the sea and the birds in the sky, over the livestock and all the wild animals, and over all the creatures that move along the ground.' So God created mankind in his own image, in the image of God he created them; male and female he created them."

Genesis 1:26-27

DEVOTION

You are not just an evolved animal or a cosmic explosion; you have been intentionally handcrafted by God to be in relationship with Him. No other being on earth has that honor. This is why we refer to God as our heavenly Father, because He created us. You have God's identity, which is why humanity carries another level of worth and value than animal or plant life. This identity is also the main thing the devil tries to attack to get you to question your value and purpose. However, you can approach every day with confidence, knowing that you are valued and loved by God.

QUESTIONS

How does it feel knowing that you were created with intention and design? What do you feel called to do?

CONFESSION

I am a child of God and am made in His image. I walk out His mission here on earth.

3

“As long as the earth endures, seed-time and harvest, cold and heat, summer and winter, day and night will never cease.”

Genesis 8:22

DEVOTION

The world God created for us is not by chance or in chaos. God's specific and intentional design holds the universe and the world in which we live in perfect harmony and peace. This is excellent news on a cosmic scale, but it also has very specific implications for your life. It's important to remember that your life isn't by chance; God has intentional plans for you. He created our world to support and provide for all life on earth until Jesus returns. You can trust Him!

QUESTIONS

Are there ever times you feel out of control or uncertain about God's plan or timing? How does it make you feel knowing God is so specific and intentional?

CONFESSION

God, you are specific and perfect in all that you do! All the principles you've established will succeed.

4

"For all have sinned and fall short of the glory of God, and all are justified freely by his grace through the redemption that came by Christ Jesus."

Romans 3:23-24

DEVOTION

Adam and Eve were the first people God made, and He gave them the choice to love and obey His Word and live or to choose death by disobeying God. They chose to disobey, and as a result, we are all born into sin. The culture says, "Everyone is basically good." While it's true that everyone is loved, we are all sinful. Only a sinless sacrifice could take away our sins. The Good News is that we are *freely* made holy through what Jesus did on the cross. We don't earn our way to God; He came and rescued us!

QUESTIONS

What was your perception of sin growing up? Did anyone tell you about needing a Savior? Have you received the grace of Jesus to cover your sin?

CONFESSION

I was born into sin, but thank God I don't have to stay in sin. I am free and forgiven because of Jesus.

5

"For God so loved the world that he gave his one and only Son, that whoever believes in him shall not perish but have eternal life."

John 3:16

DEVOTION

This is one of the most well-known verses in the world because it gives us a simple overview of how valuable we are to God and what Jesus did to provide salvation for us. Jesus left heaven and came to earth as a man to pay the price for all of humanity's sins. Jesus didn't come to earth because He was mad at our sins but because He was in love with us sinners. God gave His very best—His only Son—to rescue us. We are not an afterthought to God. Even though it was our sin that separated us, it was His grace that brought us back.

QUESTIONS

What did you think when you first heard about Jesus being willing to die in order to save you? Write down how it makes you feel to be loved that much by God.

CONFESSION

I am loved and valuable. I have put my hope and faith in Jesus!

6

"For it is by grace you have been saved, through faith—and this is not from yourselves, it is the gift of God—not by works, so that no one can boast."

Ephesians 2:8-9

DEVOTION

Your salvation from sin is not something that happens by being a good person. You may have heard that if your good deeds outweigh your bad deeds, you'll get into heaven. However, the Bible is clear that we're saved and forgiven because of the grace of God displayed on the cross. Jesus' innocent blood shed on the cross is what paid for the debt of our sins. So naturally, we want to live in a way that honors that sacrifice—but human efforts can't save you; that's why Jesus had to come!

QUESTIONS

Did you know that your good deeds don't save you? How does knowing that God paid for all your sin make you feel?

CONFESSION

I am loved and forgiven by God. His grace has saved me.

7

“If you declare with your mouth, ‘Jesus is Lord,’ and believe in your heart that God raised him from the dead, you will be saved. For it is with your heart that you believe and are justified, and it is with your mouth that you profess your faith and are saved.”

Romans 10:9-10

DEVOTION

Choosing to follow Jesus moves you from the kingdom of Satan to the kingdom of light! We are born into cruel submission to sin and the devil; all that's needed to step from darkness to light is to confess Jesus as Lord and believe what He did for you on the cross and that He rose from the dead—and you will be saved! This is incredible and kind news. It's like the thief on the cross next to Jesus; he reached out to Jesus and said, "Remember me when you come into your kingdom" (Luke 23:42), and at that moment, he was saved from darkness to light because he acknowledged Jesus as Lord.

QUESTIONS

Have you confessed that Jesus is your Lord? When did you know that Jesus was calling you? Who have you told about your decision to be a Christian?

CONFESSION

I declare that Jesus is my Lord; I will live for Him.

8

"Finally, be strong in the Lord and in his mighty power. Put on the full armor of God, so that you can take your stand against the devil's schemes. For our struggle is not against flesh and blood, but against the rulers, against the authorities, against the powers of this dark world and against the spiritual forces of evil in the heavenly realms. Therefore put on the full armor of God, so that when the day of evil comes, you may be able to stand your ground, and after you have done everything, to stand."

Ephesians 6:10-13

DEVOTION

There is a spiritual battle between demonic forces and the followers of Jesus here on earth. It's not hyperbole; it's a real battle—but the good news is that God didn't leave us without armor and weapons for this battle. Read all of Ephesians 6:10-18 to discover all of the pieces of armor. You'll notice that the armor of God is for defending and attacking. You aren't defenseless against the devil's plans to destroy you. It's important to take a stand against the enemy's attack on your life, family, city, church, and friends. When you stand up with the armor of God, you will defeat the enemy!

QUESTIONS

Have you sensed the spiritual battle? Have you had a negative demonic encounter? What's the main piece of armor that you need to focus on?

CONFESSION

I am equipped to fight and defeat the enemy.

9

“Then he said to them all: ‘Whoever wants to be my disciple must deny themselves and take up their cross daily and follow me. For whoever wants to save their life will lose it, but whoever loses their life for me will save it.’”

Luke 9:23-24

DEVOTION

Being a Christian isn't just some box you select on a religion preference survey; it's a way of life. Because He gave everything on the cross for us, we now live fully surrendered to His will and purpose. As a follower of Jesus, we lay down our life and pick up our cross to follow Jesus—daily. Don't try to save your reputation and agenda; instead, lay them down in worship to Jesus. When you surrender your whole life to Jesus, you truly start living!

QUESTIONS

Is there any part of your life you haven't yet surrendered to God? What is the greatest sacrifice that you've had to make in following Jesus?

CONFESSION

Jesus, I will lay down my life and pick up my cross daily to follow you and fulfill your mission.

10

“Is anyone among you in trouble? Let them pray. Is anyone happy? Let them sing songs of praise. Is anyone among you sick? Let them call the elders of the church to pray over them and anoint them with oil in the name of the Lord.”

James 5:13-14

DEVOTION

These verses are packed with instruction on worship, prayer, healing, and the power of the church community. We'll focus on the truth that God wants you to come to Him when you're in need. You don't have to be afraid of coming close to God; you're not bothering Him with your requests. When you pray, you enter a different kingdom where we pray instead of worry, we praise instead of fear, and we trade hopelessness for joy. Never lose your appreciation for His answered prayers.

QUESTIONS

What do you need to pray to God about today? What's one thing you're thankful for today? What miracle are you praying for today?

CONFESSION

God, I am thankful for your goodness. When I call on your name, you answer me.

11

"But seek first his kingdom and his righteousness, and all these things will be given to you as well."

Matthew 6:33

DEVOTION

God has established order and priorities within the kingdom of God, and when you put the right things in the proper order, you'll experience a greater flow and blessing. As a believer, when you shift your focus from building your own life or kingdom and start asking, "How can I build the kingdom of God with my life?" that's when your life, purpose, and dreams really begin. Initially, it will feel counterintuitive, but once you embrace a kingdom-first mindset, you'll unlock the flow of heaven. Kingdom-first means you seek God's input and direction in your life and work, and that you seek to use your resources to see people saved and discipled.

QUESTIONS

Is there anything taking greater priority in your life than God's kingdom? What area do you need to adjust focus on: time, money, or something else?

CONFESSION

I will build and advance the kingdom of God on earth with my life, work, and relationships.

12

"Having been buried with him in baptism, in which you were also raised with him through faith in the powerful working of God, who raised him from the dead."

Colossians 2:12 (ESV)

DEVOTION

Jesus was baptized in water, and we're called to follow His example and get water baptized as well. This means to be fully submerged underneath the water. Why? Because this act symbolically represents Jesus' death, burial, and resurrection. When we get baptized, we publicly claim Jesus and commit to living fully surrendered to Him. Your life is not your own; you're living for His kingdom and His purpose.

QUESTIONS

Have you taken the step to get water baptized yet? If yes, what was it like? Is there any area of your life you need to surrender today?

CONFESSION

I am a follower of Jesus. I am dead to my old life of sin and alive to Jesus and His purpose!

13

"Here I am! I stand at the door and knock. If anyone hears my voice and opens the door, I will come in and eat with that person, and they with me."

Revelation 3:20

DEVOTION

In this verse, Jesus gives you a window into the heart of God for you. First, Jesus wants to come into your life. He doesn't want to stay as a distant spectator; He wants to be personally engaged in your world. He also explains that you have to invite Him in. He's knocking on the door; only you can choose to open it. And once you open the door, He says, "I'll come in and share a meal with you." He doesn't just want to give you a salvation ticket to heaven and move on to the next door. He wants to stay and share a meal with you. That's the heart of God: to be with you!

QUESTIONS

Have you invited Jesus into your heart? If not, today is an incredible day for it. Do you create space in your day to spend time with God?

CONFESSION

Jesus, you are welcome into every area of my life.

14

"Shout for joy to the LORD, all the earth. Worship the LORD with gladness; come before him with joyful songs. Know that the LORD is God. It is he who made us, and we are his; we are his people, the sheep of his pasture. Enter his gates with thanksgiving and his courts with praise; give thanks to him and praise his name. For the LORD is good and his love endures forever; his faithfulness continues through all generations."

Psalm 100:1-5

DEVOTION

You'll find that when you come to God in worship and with a thankful heart, it brings you right into His presence. Worship, praise, and thankfulness are like a special access code to heaven. That's the foundation of honor that so much of the kingdom of God is built on. Do you have a heart of thankfulness for all He's done in your life? God does want to hear all your requests, needs, pains, and victories. But what is the first thing we bring to God: our complaints or our praise?

QUESTIONS

How comfortable are you in worship? Have you taken the step to worship and sing in church? Reflect on who God is and praise Him this week.

CONFESSION

I will worship and honor God with everything that is within me.

15

“Jesus replied: ‘Love the Lord your God with all your heart and with all your soul and with all your mind.’ This is the first and greatest commandment. And the second is like it: ‘Love your neighbor as yourself.’”

Matthew 22:37-39

DEVOTION

Jesus makes it very simple and clear as to what are the most important things we should know and do as a believer. First is to love God fully and passionately with all you have. How do we do that? By loving God with our work, with our family, with our dreams, and with everything. Then it's to love others. God makes it clear that we can't just love God and mistreat people. To love God is also to love His kids. Loving others the way God loves you is key to how we love Him.

QUESTIONS

What areas of your life do you have an easier time committing to God? What areas do you struggle to love God with? Are there any people you need to express greater love toward in your life?

CONFESSION

I will love God with every part of my life, and I will love others selflessly.

16

"For if you forgive other people when they sin against you, your heavenly Father will also forgive you. But if you do not forgive others their sins, your Father will not forgive your sins."

Matthew 6:14-15

DEVOTION

Forgiveness is one of the primary hallmarks of Christianity. Because Jesus forgave us fully and completely of our sins, He requires that we forgive others. While we didn't earn our salvation or have to work for it, there is an expectation from God that we extend grace to others as He extended it to us. When you have difficulty letting go of what someone did to you, take time to pray and remember His goodness toward you. Ask God for peace and help to extend grace toward others. It's not about them deserving your forgiveness, just as we didn't deserve or earn Jesus' forgiveness.

QUESTIONS

Who in your life do you need to forgive today? How have you learned to overcome offenses?

CONFESSION

I have been forgiven and will extend grace to others.

17

"And without faith it is impossible to please God, because anyone who comes to him must believe that he exists and that he rewards those who earnestly seek him."

Hebrews 11:6

DEVOTION

Without faith, it's impossible to please God. Faith is the currency of heaven. It's the conduit for bringing things from heaven to earth. It pleases God because faith is believing He is who He says He is, and it's drawing on Him in faith for the unseen or the impossible. God wants you to come to Him with great expectation. Never feel like you're asking God for too much. Instead, pray and believe for that miracle, and trust Him to fulfill it. Pray like He's about to answer your prayer!

QUESTIONS

When was the last time you prayed a bold prayer of faith? What prayer did you stop praying because of fear that you need to start believing for again?

CONFESSION

God, I trust you and put my faith in you. You will fulfill what you said you would do.

18

“Do not conform to the pattern of this world, but be transformed by the renewing of your mind. Then you will be able to test and approve what God’s will is—his good, pleasing and perfect will.”

Romans 12:2

DEVOTION

Every day you have a choice as to what pattern you're going to model your life after. Will it be the pattern of the world leading to death? Or will it be the pattern of God—found in the Bible—that leads to life? As you follow Jesus and His ways, your life will be transformed little by little. God's Word has a pattern to build great friendships, marriages, businesses, governments, and each area of our lives. The key is to stay committed to following God's pattern even when you feel you'd rather follow the world's pattern. Only one leads to life.

QUESTIONS

What's a key pattern of thinking or doing that's changed in your life since becoming a Christian? What's one negative pattern you want God to transform in your life?

CONFESSION

I will build my life on the pattern of God's Word. I will know and fulfill God's will for my life.

19

"Blessed is the one who does not walk in step with the wicked or stand in the way that sinners take or sit in the company of mockers, but whose delight is in the law of the LORD, and who meditates on his law day and night. That person is like a tree planted by streams of water, which yields its fruit in season and whose leaf does not wither—whatever they do prospers."

Psalm 1:1-3

DEVOTION

These verses end by letting you know that God's desire is that you would produce fruit and that you would prosper. But so much of that hinges on who you allow into your world and what counsel you let in. Who are you walking with? Who are you sitting with? Be very intentional with the friends and associates you allow to speak into your life. The direction of our closest friends will impact the direction of our lives. So, observe the fruit or attitudes in people before you choose to listen to their counsel.

QUESTIONS

Who are the closest friends or mentors speaking life into you? Is there anyone that you need to remove from your inner circle?

CONFESSION

I will walk with those who prioritize God's ways. I will prosper and thrive in every season.

20

"Therefore everyone who hears these words of mine and puts them into practice is like a wise man who built his house on the rock. The rain came down, the streams rose, and the winds blew and beat against that house; yet it did not fall, because it had its foundation on the rock. But everyone who hears these words of mine and does not put them into practice is like a foolish man who built his house on sand. The rain came down, the streams rose, and the winds blew and beat against that house, and it fell with a great crash."

Matthew 7:24-27

DEVOTION

What foundation are you building your life on? Jesus calls us to build on the only sure and solid foundation, which is His Word. Following the ideas and thoughts from this world is like building your house on a shaky and uncertain foundation. Your life, like a house, can only stand when it's built on a rock-solid foundation. If you've been building on the lies of culture, the good news is you can change that by reading, listening to, and obeying the Bible in a way that will build your sure foundation.

QUESTIONS

Is there any area of your life that seems to be falling apart and needs to be rebuilt on the foundation of God's Word? What Bible verses will you commit to memorize?

CONFESSION

My life will be built on the foundation of God's Word.

21

“But you will receive power when the Holy Spirit comes on you; and you will be my witnesses in Jerusalem, and in all Judea and Samaria, and to the ends of the earth.”

Acts 1:8

DEVOTION

Jesus didn't just save us from sin and leave us powerless on our own; He sent us the Holy Spirit. When you are filled and baptized with the Holy Spirit, you'll receive power, peace, wisdom, and all the fruit of the Spirit. The Bible calls the Holy Spirit our counselor, guide, comforter, and the one who gives us power. Through the Holy Spirit, we can operate in power and authority in Jesus' name. He also empowers us to be His witnesses on earth so that many more can come to salvation in Jesus. Ask Jesus today to baptize you with the Holy Spirit and power!

QUESTIONS

Have you been baptized with the Holy Spirit yet? How has it changed your life? Who can you share your faith with this week?

CONFESSION

I am filled with the Holy Spirit and will share my faith.

22

"Whoever can be trusted with very little can also be trusted with much, and whoever is dishonest with very little will also be dishonest with much."

Luke 16:10

DEVOTION

One of the vital principles of promotion in life is to be faithful with what you have now, even if it's not much. God is good and doesn't want to bless you beyond what you are ready for, so He'll watch how you handle "little" before you're promoted to "much." Sometimes we assume that once we're given more or blessed with more, then we'll begin to level up our faithfulness with what we have, but God waits and watches how you care for the current friends you have or the job you have or the home you have or what you've done with the calling He's given you so far; based on that, you'll see the blessing of God!

QUESTIONS

How are you currently handling what you have? Are you multiplying what you've been given?

CONFESSION

I will be faithful and multiply what I am given.

23

"I have hidden your word in my heart that I might not sin against you."

Psalm 119:11

DEVOTION

When you put God's Word into your heart, it has a way of guarding, insulating, and protecting your life against the enemy. The way that you hide God's Word in your heart is by reading it often—daily if you can—and deciding what you're going to apply from what you just read. Another great way is to choose key verses, like the ones in this book, to memorize. Then when you're faced with difficult moments, the Holy Spirit will bring those verses to memory, and they will be a guard against the enemy.

QUESTIONS

What's your favorite verse in the Bible so far? When can you plan daily to read the Bible? Check out reading plans on the Following Jesus app.

CONFESSION

Your Word guards, protects, and guides my life.

24

“Come to me, all you who are weary and burdened, and I will give you rest.”

Matthew 11:28

DEVOTION

What an incredible invitation from Jesus! When you face difficulty, pain, tragedy, fatigue, bad news, or anything burdening to you, Jesus says to come to Him! You don't have to carry everything alone; you can bring it all to Jesus. What is your default when you face difficulty? Do you run to God and His Word, or do you turn inward and try to carry it all? Or do you turn to other vices to numb the pain? Get good at consistently bringing your fears and worries to God, and watch how your peace and joy return.

QUESTIONS

What's the biggest thing burdening you right now? What fears are trying to mess with your peace? How can you bring this to Jesus?

CONFESSION

I will bring my worries and fears to Jesus in exchange for His peace and strength.

25

"For I received from the Lord what I also passed on to you: The Lord Jesus, on the night he was betrayed, took bread, and when he had given thanks, he broke it and said, 'This is my body, which is for you; do this in remembrance of me.' In the same way, after supper he took the cup, saying, 'This cup is the new covenant in my blood; do this, whenever you drink it, in remembrance of me.'"

1 Corinthians 11:23-25

DEVOTION

Jesus calls us to take communion consistently. What is that? It's when you eat bread and drink wine or juice to represent what Jesus did for us on the cross. The church you go to may have the whole church take communion often, and you can also practice this on your own. But I want to encourage you not to take that moment lightly; it is a powerful declaration of the power of the blood of Jesus over your life and circumstances. It's the blood of Jesus that saves, heals, covers, and protects you. When facing oppression from the enemy, take communion and stand against his attack.

QUESTIONS

How has taking communion impacted your life? What is the most impactful part of Jesus' sacrifice on the cross?

CONFESSION

Jesus, your blood heals and covers my life.

26

"By this everyone will know that you are my disciples, if you love one another."

John 13:35

DEVOTION

Your faith isn't supposed to be hidden or silent. There are many ways that our faith is made public, and how you love others is one of those key factors. When a non-believer sees the way you love them and the love the people in your church have for each other, it's a massive testimony to them. The world bases love on performance and what others can do for you, but as believers, we love and receive everyone—which is so shocking, it attracts people to want to follow Jesus!

QUESTIONS

Do you have close Christian friends? Are you displaying the love of God in the ways you treat and connect with your friends?

CONFESSION

I will live a life of love! I will love, honor, and encourage my friends and those in my world.

27

"When the day of Pentecost came, they were all together in one place. Suddenly a sound like the blowing of a violent wind came from heaven and filled the whole house where they were sitting. They saw what seemed to be tongues of fire that separated and came to rest on each of them. All of them were filled with the Holy Spirit and began to speak in other tongues as the Spirit enabled them."

Acts 2:1-4

DEVOTION

The Holy Spirit is not just some little voice on your shoulder trying to help you make better decisions; He is the Spirit of God! The Holy Spirit wants to empower and fill your life. Notice how the disciples were in unity and prayer, waiting for the Lord to send them the promised gift of comfort, help, and power. The Holy Spirit goes where He's invited. So, wait on and ask for the leading and power of the Holy Spirit and begin to step into your day with confidence and authority that God's Spirit is with you.

QUESTIONS

When was the last time you spent time in worship seeking God? In church or at home? Invite the Holy Spirit to fill you! Have you felt a difference in your boldness since being filled with the Holy Spirit?

CONFESSION

Holy Spirit, I invite you to come and fill every area of my life.

28

“Two are better than one, because they have a good return for their labor: If either of them falls down, one can help the other up. But pity anyone who falls and has no one to help them up. Also, if two lie down together, they will keep warm. But how can one keep warm alone? Though one may be overpowered, two can defend themselves. A cord of three strands is not quickly broken.”

Ecclesiastes 4:9-12

DEVOTION

We are designed by God for relationships. Having great people in your life isn't just a nice idea; it's essential for your development and for fulfilling your purpose and calling. Don't try to be an island in life; don't try to do it all alone. Find people you can link arms with and go after your purpose. This is important in your times of need, but it's also so that you can position yourself as the friend someone else will need. Yes, there may be times when life feels faster on your own, but if you want to go the distance, it will require friends.

QUESTIONS

When have you fallen and had a great friend help you back up? Who do you need or want to build a friendship with?

CONFESSION

My life is stronger and more fulfilling with friends. I will serve and add value to others.

29

"Come near to God and he will come near to you. Wash your hands, you sinners, and purify your hearts, you double-minded."

James 4:8

DEVOTION

What an incredible invitation to all of us! The Creator of the heavens and the earth has called us to be close to Him. You don't need to be religious or distant. Instead, come close to God. How do we do this? We get close to God by spending time with Him. We can spend time with God in prayer, in worship, and by reading the Bible. You'll find that as you step closer to God, the presence and power of God will meet you and give you strength.

QUESTIONS

Is there anything stopping you from spending time with Jesus? What is your favorite way to spend time with God?

CONFESSION

My heavenly Father wants to be close to me. I will chase after His presence.

30

"But whatever were gains to me I now consider loss for the sake of Christ. What is more, I consider everything a loss because of the surpassing worth of knowing Christ Jesus my Lord, for whose sake I have lost all things. I consider them garbage, that I may gain Christ."

Philippians 3:7-8

DEVOTION

There's nothing that compares to our ability to be in a relationship with God. No matter how many great accomplishments you might have over your life so far, remember that none of that earns your way to salvation; it's only what Jesus has done that matters. So, like the Apostle Paul, choose Christ and the life He has for you over all earthly possessions. Nothing else will satisfy and bring fulfillment to your life like knowing Jesus!

QUESTIONS

Was there anything you had to give up when you came to Christ? What's the greatest accomplishment you've achieved from an earthly perspective?

CONFESSION

I surrender all of me to follow Jesus. Nothing is greater or more valuable than Him!

31

"I have told you these things, so that in me you may have peace. In this world you will have trouble. But take heart! I have overcome the world."

John 16:33

DEVOTION

Becoming a Christian won't necessarily make your life easier; there will always be trouble in our world because of sin. Yes, there is a lot of self-inflicted pain that we begin to avoid as we live according to the Bible. However, because Satan is still roaming the earth, there are going to be attacks that we need to be aware of and know how to deal with. Jesus says, "You'll have trouble, but take heart or have courage and peace because I've already won the victory!" Now, all we need to do is fight the battle.

QUESTIONS

Are you more naturally stressed out or at peace in life? What's the battle you're fighting right now that God is helping you overcome?

CONFESSION

No matter what trouble comes my way, I have peace and walk in the victory Jesus has already won.

32

"Therefore I tell you, whatever you ask for in prayer, believe that you have received it, and it will be yours."

Mark 11:24

DEVOTION

Through Jesus, we see God's heart to engage and respond to us. First, He calls us to pray and ask Him for things. Don't assume you're bothering God, because your heavenly Father loves you and wants to respond. Then Jesus calls us to the next level by challenging us to believe. The fight for answered prayers is in the believing! Most things you ask God for will be contested by the devil and delays. Can we keep trusting God and believe He will do what He says even when the natural circumstances don't look good?

QUESTIONS

What are you praying and believing God for right now? Is there any prayer or dream God has given you that you've lost heart and stopped believing for?

CONFESSION

In faith, I will boldly ask God for my needs and desires.

33

"Then Jesus came to them and said, 'All authority in heaven and on earth has been given to me. Therefore go and make disciples of all nations, baptizing them in the name of the Father and of the Son and of the Holy Spirit, and teaching them to obey everything I have commanded you. And surely I am with you always, to the very end of the age.'"

Matthew 28:18-20

DEVOTION

As followers of Jesus, we're not just here taking up space; we're on a mission. The mandate to increase and take dominion began in the Garden of Eden with Adam and Eve, but Jesus calls us back to that mission when He says to make and increase disciples on the earth. There are people that God has put around us who need the message of salvation through Jesus. We know that Jesus does the saving, and then it's our responsibility to do the discipling, which is to teach people how to obey and follow Jesus and make more disciples.

QUESTIONS

Who has had a significant impact on your faith so far? Find and identify three people that you can disciple. If you have kids, they're your first disciples. Who are you inviting to come to church with you?

CONFESSION

I will own the great commission from Jesus to make disciples of all nations, starting with my family and close friends.

34

"The thief comes only to steal and kill and destroy; I have come that they may have life, and have it to the full."

John 10:10

DEVOTION

The signature of God is life! When you're trying to determine if God is involved in something, look for signs of life. The enemy will continue to take from you; he'll try to kill your life, your potential, and your hope. His tactics will be mostly subtle. He won't come in and try to get you to accept his poison, but he'll try to get you to think and speak thoughts and words of death. This scripture is also a way to reflect on your attitudes and actions to see if they are flowing from God or the enemy. Is what you're doing in your life producing life or death in others around you?

QUESTIONS

Is there any area of your life that keeps producing death? How has following Jesus changed your life?

CONFESSION

Jesus, all your ways produce life—life to the full.

35

“All this energy issues from Christ: God raised him from death and set him on a throne in deep heaven, in charge of running the universe, everything from galaxies to governments, no name and no power exempt from his rule. And not just for the time being, but *forever*. He is in charge of it all, has the final word on everything. At the center of all this, Christ rules the church. The church, you see, is not peripheral to the world; the world is peripheral to the church. The church is Christ’s body, in which he speaks and acts, by which he fills everything with his presence.”

Ephesians 1:20-23 (MSG)

DEVOTION

Jesus is powerfully active on the earth today through the Church. The gathering of believers at church is not just a religious gathering but the active body and extension of Jesus here on earth! You are an essential part of the body of Jesus and His plan to seek and save the planet. Jesus has chosen to primarily speak and act through His Church on earth. While we go to a church weekly to worship and hear the teaching of God's Word, we don't just *go* to church—we *are* the Church. So, be ready to be used by God to speak, act, and extend His kingdom through your life.

QUESTIONS

What church are you a part of, and how can you be more involved? How can you share Jesus with those around you?

CONFESSION

I am a vital part of the Church, fulfilling the mission Jesus gave us to accomplish.

36

“This, then, is how you should pray: ‘Our Father in heaven, hallowed be your name, your kingdom come, your will be done, on earth as it is in heaven. Give us today our daily bread. And forgive us our debts, as we also have forgiven our debtors. And lead us not into temptation, but deliver us from the evil one.’”

Matthew 6:9-13

DEVOTION

If you feel unsure how to pray, you're in good company. The disciples asked Jesus to teach them how to pray, and these verses were His response. Jesus gives several specifics, but a few key highlights are coming to God with honor and worship, and believing that you are called to be part of bringing heaven to earth. Jesus highlights our need to forgive others and points us to ask God for what we need, teaching us to come to God as our Father and not as a distant religious deity. Come confidently to God, knowing He's ready to listen and respond.

QUESTIONS

How do you like to pray? What's the greatest thing you've seen happen after you prayed?

CONFESSION

I will boldly approach my heavenly Father. Lord, your will be done on earth as it is in heaven.

37

**"Your word is a lamp for my feet,
a light on my path."**

Psalm 119:105

DEVOTION

In this life, we can sometimes feel confused or uncertain about the next steps we should take. But that's where God's Word comes in. The Bible can act as a sort of flashlight on the path of life. When we have the Bible closed, we will stumble in the darkness and trip over things because we can't see. But when we open the Bible, it floods our life with light so we can see clearly. Most often, the confusion in the world and in our lives personally is because we don't have God's Word lighting up our next step.

QUESTIONS

How do you approach reading the Bible? Have you started a daily Bible reading plan? When has the Bible shed light on a decision you needed to make?

CONFESSION

God's Word brings light and clarity to my daily decisions.

38

“Do nothing out of selfish ambition or vain conceit. Rather, in humility value others above yourselves, not looking to your own interests but each of you to the interests of the others.”

Philippians 2:3-4

DEVOTION

These verses "hurt so good." They are powerful in their effect on your life, but they require an initial step of self-sacrifice that is often uncomfortable or unnatural. Most of life's challenges come from not applying this scripture. God designed life to work best when you stop focusing on yourself and focus more on meeting the needs of others. But, the spirit of this world wants you to make life all about you. This can even sound like wisdom sometimes, but it doesn't work because God created the world to work best when we serve others just as He served us.

QUESTIONS

How can you focus more on serving others? What's one area of your life where you've been selfish? Surrender that to God right now and ask Him to help you seek humility instead.

CONFESSION

I will focus on serving others' needs before my own.

39

"For the love of money is a root of all kinds of evil. Some people, eager for money, have wandered from the faith and pierced themselves with many griefs. But you, man of God, flee from all this, and pursue righteousness, godliness, faith, love, endurance and gentleness."

1 Timothy 6:10-11

DEVOTION

Money is a massive part of our lives because it fuels how we live, build the economy, and engage with others. Money can be incredibly helpful, but it can also corrupt and destroy. From these verses, we see the issue isn't money but the *love* of it. The key here is found at the end of the last verse: pursue righteousness and love. Use money to pursue all that God has given you, rather than using what God has given you to pursue money and its trappings. A primary way to stay free from the love of money is to stay generous. Give often and give generously!

QUESTIONS

Do you have a hard time being generous with money? When is the last time you helped a local outreach or a friend in need without expecting repayment?

CONFESSION

I will be generous with all God has blessed me with.

40

"It is God's will that you should be sanctified: that you should avoid sexual immorality; that each of you should learn to control your own body in a way that is holy and honorable, not in passionate lust like the pagans, who do not know God."

1 Thessalonians 4:3-5

DEVOTION

The world tries to tell us that we need to follow our impulses and desires, but God gives us the Holy Spirit to help produce self-control. Because of our sinful nature, we'll often be pulled toward sin. Instead of giving in, we—by the power of God and courage—rise above to do what is right according to God's Word versus doing what feels right according to the world and our instincts. This includes our sexuality. We must honor God with how we handle ourselves sexually. We're called to save sex for marriage, and nothing outside of sex between a man and woman is acceptable to God and His design.

QUESTIONS

Did you know that God cares about what you do with your body? Are there any practices that you need to change in order to honor God?

CONFESSION

I will honor God with my whole heart, mind, and body, and set my heart to live in sexual purity from now on.

41

**"Lazy hands make for poverty,
but diligent hands bring wealth."**

Proverbs 10:4

DEVOTION

While God loves you and wants to bless your life in many ways, that doesn't mean He will just give you everything you want. His blessing is on the work of our hands. When we're faithful, diligent, effective, and productive, God's blessing will be on that! When we're lazy and assume the world owes us something or think that God should do all the work, we will come to poverty. No matter where you find yourself financially, you can rise up by applying God's wealth principles found in the Bible. God won't get behind laziness, but He accelerates hard work.

QUESTIONS

Are you diligent with your work? Is there a way you can increase your value at your job or begin a new business?

CONFESSION

I will honor God by being faithful, diligent, and committed to my work.

42

“Peter and the other apostles replied: ‘We must obey God rather than human beings!’”

Acts 5:29

DEVOTION

While God calls us to love, serve, and prefer others above ourselves, there are times when you have to go against what others are saying, even when they are your authority. The disciples knew that if the word of the government ever contradicted the Word of God, they had to choose God over man. Being a Christian means that you should carry more kindness and love than others, but it doesn't mean that you do whatever you're told. It means you live by a moral code and convictions that drive you toward truth.

QUESTIONS

Is there any command your government or boss has given you that causes you to ignore your biblical morality? How can you stand up to evil?

CONFESSION

I will obey God and speak the truth, even when it's inconvenient or even if I am persecuted.

43

"'Will a mere mortal rob God? Yet you rob me. But you ask, "How are we robbing you?" In tithes and offerings. You are under a curse—your whole nation—because you are robbing me. Bring the whole tithe into the storehouse, that there may be food in my house. Test me in this,' says the LORD Almighty, 'and see if I will not throw open the floodgates of heaven and pour out so much blessing that there will not be room enough to store it.'"

Malachi 3:8-10

DEVOTION

Tithing is a practice that God calls us to commit to, which is bringing God the first 10 percent of all we earn. This is about priorities, trust, and God's economy. God doesn't need our money; He wants our hearts and our trust. When we bring the first portion of our income to Him, it allows God to test how well we trust Him. And when we give in this way, God promises to open the windows of heaven and pour out blessings in abundance. When we engage in giving, we are opening up the kingdom flow of giving and receiving.

QUESTIONS

Have you heard of tithing before? Have you started tithing 10 percent to your church?

CONFESSION

I will trust God in my giving and see His blessing in my life. I am blessed so I can be a blessing!

44

"Finally, brothers and sisters, whatever is true, whatever is noble, whatever is right, whatever is pure, whatever is lovely, whatever is admirable—if anything is excellent or praiseworthy—think about such things."

Philippians 4:8

DEVOTION

This is one of the greatest formulas in the Bible that will unlock God's best for you. Learning to shift and choose what you consistently focus on will transform your life. Our thoughts are a primary driver of our emotions and our actions. So, what you focus on will determine where your life ends up. Will it be in strength, peace, and blessing? Or will you end up in pain, loneliness, and dysfunction? It primarily depends on focusing on this list from Philippians 4:8 in your life, relationships, and calling—those qualities that are true, noble, right, pure, lovely, admirable, excellent, and praiseworthy.

QUESTIONS

Do you tend to lean toward positivity or negativity? What areas of your life would improve if you started thinking about the things listed in this verse and speaking life?

CONFESSION

I will choose to focus on what is good.

45

"But you, dear friends, by building yourselves up in your most holy faith and praying in the Holy Spirit, keep yourselves in God's love as you wait for the mercy of our Lord Jesus Christ to bring you to eternal life."

Jude 20-21

DEVOTION

Our relationship with Jesus is a journey that grows during our whole lives. We aren't fully mature in our faith when we get saved, just like we're not fully mature when we're initially born. Growth is a process, and one of those key growth catalysts is the Holy Spirit, specifically praying in the Spirit. All the difficult pressures and pains in life can cloud our judgment or overwhelm us, but God's Word says that praying in the Holy Spirit builds us up in a unique way so that we can overcome anything coming against us.

QUESTIONS

Have you made praying in the Spirit a daily habit? Did you know that God wants your faith to grow? What has the Holy Spirit been speaking to you about?

CONFESSION

I will build up my faith as I pray in the Spirit.

46

"So Christ himself gave the apostles, the prophets, the evangelists, the pastors and teachers, to equip his people for works of service, so that the body of Christ may be built up until we all reach unity in the faith and in the knowledge of the Son of God and become mature, attaining to the whole measure of the fullness of Christ."

Ephesians 4:11-13

DEVOTION

God is Spirit, but He's not chaos. God established order, government, and leadership in everything He created—in heaven, in the nations, in families, and in the church. While all believers are equal in love and value to God, He has called some to step into primary leadership roles within the Church. These are listed in Ephesians 4:11-13. You may be called by God to carry out one of those roles. If you do, lead with courage and grace. If you're called to follow one of those primary leaders, follow with honor and grace.

QUESTIONS

Do you feel called by God to one of the five primary church leadership roles? How are you currently serving at your church?

CONFESSION

I will honor those whom God calls to lead His Church. When called, I will lead with humility and courage.

47

"But the fruit of the Spirit is love, joy, peace, forbearance, kindness, goodness, faithfulness, gentleness and self-control. Against such things there is no law. Those who belong to Christ Jesus have crucified the flesh with its passions and desires. Since we live by the Spirit, let us keep in step with the Spirit."

Galatians 5:22-25

DEVOTION

Fruit is the product of a seed. In the same way, when we open up our lives and hearts to the Spirit of God, He'll plant seeds of love, joy, peace, and all the qualities mentioned in Galatians 5:22-23. As we keep cultivating these seeds, we'll find they begin to produce that same life in us. From the beginning, God made seeds to produce after their kind. So, when you plant seeds from the world, they will produce death; when you plant seeds of the Spirit from God's Word, they will produce life!

QUESTIONS

What seeds are you planting in your life right now? Are they from the Spirit or from the flesh?

CONFESSION

I will walk in step with the Holy Spirit. As I follow the Holy Spirit, I'll see the fruit of the Spirit in my life.

48

“For if you remain silent at this time, relief and deliverance for the Jews will arise from another place, but you and your father’s family will perish. And who knows but that you have come to your royal position for such a time as this?”

Esther 4:14

DEVOTION

If you're breathing, then you have a purpose! Take Esther's story to heart: the challenges you see around you are not there just for you to feel sad about or just for you to pray about; maybe God positioned you in your workplace, neighborhood, school, or nation for such a time as this. As followers of Jesus, we're not called to stick our heads in the sand and ignore the issues around us; we've been sent on assignment to be the solution. If you're passionate or frustrated about something in the world, it's most likely because God is calling you to be part of the solution.

QUESTIONS

What frustrates or saddens you the most in the world right now? Is there something you can do to change it?

CONFESSION

I am positioned for such a time as this. I won't be silent. I will engage and transform my world.

49

"And we know that in all things God works for the good of those who love him, who have been called according to his purpose."

Romans 8:28

DEVOTION

Not all things are good, and not all of the storms are from God—but He does promise us that in every and all circumstances, He is working it for our good. He will allow us to fight battles and go through difficulty, but He will never waste the pain we're going through. Hold on to this truth like it's a weapon to defeat the enemy. The devil will try to discourage you and get you to think you're defeated, but trust God, keep doing what's right, and watch God work out your story for His good!

QUESTIONS

Reflect on a time when God worked good out of your pain and tragedy. What might God be doing right now through your current trials?

CONFESSION

God is good, and He is working all things for my good!

50

“As Jesus was getting into the boat, the man who had been demon-possessed begged to go with him. Jesus did not let him, but said, ‘Go home to your own people and tell them how much the Lord has done for you, and how he has had mercy on you.’”

Mark 5:18-19

DEVOTION

God has saved you and set you free, and now it's your turn to go into your world and tell others the story of the goodness of God. Many people in your world may not come to church initially, but you can still share about how Jesus has impacted your life. You may feel like you're not qualified to share your faith or lead someone to Jesus, but this man who was set free had no training; he simply had an encounter with Jesus. He was a witness to what Jesus did in his life. That's the main thing that Jesus is asking from you—to tell your story!

QUESTIONS

How has Jesus changed your life? Who can you tell your story to this week? Who can you invite to church?

CONFESSION

I will tell the story of God's goodness and salvation in my life to the people around me.

51

"As for other matters, brothers and sisters, we instructed you how to live in order to please God, as in fact you are living. Now we ask you and urge you in the Lord Jesus to do this more and more."

1 Thessalonians 4:1

DEVOTION

The more you walk with Jesus, the more you'll want to please Him with your life. It's not something you'll feel obligated to do; it's just the natural response to His grace and goodness in your life. I love how the Apostle Paul calls us to take what we've been learning and keep growing more and more. Don't stop and settle for your current level of maturity. This verse also reminds us that most of our faith journey won't be a lot of new things, but a deepening of our understanding and a strengthening of the fundamentals of our faith.

QUESTIONS

What are a few of the key fundamentals of following Jesus you've learned so far? What's one area you could grow in right now?

CONFESSION

I will keep growing in my faith and live to please God.

52

"The seventh angel sounded his trumpet, and there were loud voices in heaven, which said: 'The kingdom of the world has become the kingdom of our Lord and of his Messiah, and he will reign for ever and ever.'"

Revelation 11:15

DEVOTION

As we wrap up this book, it's important to know that God has an ultimate plan to evict evil from the earth and reestablish His kingdom across the planet! Jesus won our salvation on the cross, and He will have the final victory over the devil and end his rule on earth once and for all. When this time comes, all nations will submit to Jesus as our ultimate King and ruler. There will be no tribe or nation that's outside of His rule. So you can rest in God's plan and have great hope knowing that no matter what we face in our lifetime, God will bring judgment to Satan and restore the earth.

QUESTIONS

Are you confident in the future? How are you working to establish His kingdom on earth until He comes back?

CONFESSION

There is one King, and His name is Jesus. He will reign and restore all the nations of the earth to Himself.

About the Author

Samuel is a passionate follower of Jesus, in love with his beautiful wife, Katie, and loves being a father to his two incredible girls, Mercedes and Kenzie. He and his wife are a part of the pastoral team at Awaken Church in San Diego, California. They also serve the broader Church community by preaching and teaching, and through the discipleship resource called *Following Jesus.*